JUST PRAY!

a book of poetic prayers
and prayerful poems

To Martha & John,
whose friendship I
treasure —

May God's grace, love,
peace and joy be yours

Jonetta

JUST PRAY!
a book of poetic prayers
and prayerful poems

JORETTA K. KLEPFER

TATE PUBLISHING & *Enterprises*

"Just Pray!" by Joretta K. Klepfer
Copyright © 2006 by Joretta K. Klepfer.

All rights reserved.
Published in the United States of America
by Tate Publishing, LLC
127 East Trade Center Terrace
Mustang, OK 73064 (888) 361-9473

Book design copyright © 2006 by Tate Publishing, LLC. All rights reserved.

No part of this publication may be reproduced, stored in a retrieval system or transmitted in any way by any means, electronic, mechanical, photocopy, recording or otherwise without the prior permission of the author except as provided by USA copyright law.

All Scripture taken from the Holy Bible, New International Version *,
Copyright © 1973, 1978, 1984 by International Bible Society. Used by permission of Zondervan Publishing House. All rights reserved.

Cover Designed by Rusty Eldred
Layout Designed by Melissa Griggs
ISBN: 1-5988650-9-9
260803

Dedicated
to the Glory of God

In Honor of

Margaret H. Kennerly
My Mother, My Mentor, My Friend

Robert O. Klepfer, Jr. (Bob)
My Husband, My Soul Mate, My Friend

Robert O. Klepfer, III (B3)
My Son, My Consultant, My Friend

I thank my God every time I remember you. In all my prayers for all of you, I always pray with joy because of your partnership in the gospel from the first day until now, being confident of this, that he who began a good work in you will carry it to completion until the day of Jesus Christ.

Philippians 1:3-6

Thank You

I am truly grateful for faithful family and friends who read the first draft and who have encouraged me not only during this book project but also throughout my life.

Bob Klepfer, Jr.	Bob Klepfer, III
Dana McIver	Pastor Brady Faggart
Pastor Charlie Zimmerman	June & John Witherspoon
Ruth Roland	Betty Masters
Carol & Rick Diehl	Sherrie Harmon
Pat Bergen	Anna Mercedes
Bishop Leonard H. Bolick	

A special thank you goes to Dana McIver, who coordinated the first draft "blind reading" to provide an opportunity for anonymous responses.

The second draft was almost double in length, so I am especially grateful to the following friends and family who reviewed it and provided invaluable advice:

Marshall Hurley	Kathleen Brinkey
Dana McIver	Ellenor Shepherd
Matthew McIver	Clarence Smith
Bob Klepfer, Jr.	Bob Klepfer, III

I am deeply appreciative of the strong foundation in the English language and in writing that I received through the school system at Mooresville, North Carolina. I am indeed grateful to Martha Lippard Smith, my high school English teacher, not only for her teaching long ago, but also her gracious offer of editorial assistance with this book.

Thank you, Bishop Bolick and Dana McIver, for your kind words of endorsement as well as your friendship and personal encouragement.

My husband, Bob, has blessed me with strong encouragement, editing assistance and support—both literal and emotional. My son, Bob III (aka B3), has blessed me with technical support as my long distance computer consultant, as well as with advice and encouragement. "Thank you" is not enough, but I offer it with much love and great joy.

Just Pray!

In the beginning ...

Dear Readers:

I am a child of God, a wife, and a mother. A lifelong Lutheran, my greatest joys come from faith, family and friends.

Several years ago, I began a genuine effort to give God the first minutes of the day by spending time in prayer and reading the Bible and other inspirational books. I tried journaling with questionable success. When I attended a spirituality retreat in January 1998, I noticed that my journal writing kept producing poetry. Throughout the following months and years, when inspiration seemed to be present, so were my pen and paper.

During the first 55 years of my life, although I enjoyed poetry immensely, I wrote only a very few poems (probably fewer than five). I have to assume God has his reasons for this sudden onset of inspired verse and intends that these poems be shared in some fashion.

The NIV Scripture passages complete the message of the poem/prayer. Some inspired the poem; others were called to mind after the poem was written. The greatest effect is accomplished by prayerful attention to both.

I hope you enjoy this book, and I pray that it will inspire you to set aside time for God each day to enjoy his presence and listen to his message for you.

May your life be blessed by your time in prayer.

Yours in Christ,
Joretta K. Klepfer

Just Pray!

Invitation

These verses all come from daily visits with
    God, Creator
        Jesus, Savior
            Spirit, Sanctifier.

May you find what you need as you read:
    His joy in your life,
        His love always present,
            His peace in your heart,
But especially ...
    a connection with God;
    a conviction to spend time just being together with him;
    a heart open to hearing his word for you;
    a willingness to let God have control of your life
        and trust in the outcome;
    courage to turn loose of your own will to follow his;
    an awareness each day of his constant love
        and presence with you;
    a belief that God answers your prayer, even
        if it's not the answer you want.
As you read and enjoy each verse, may you be
    Surrounded by God's love,
        Immersed in his peace,
            Delighted by his joy!

THIS IS THE STUFF OF FAITH!
    OF DISCIPLESHIP!
        OF A RELATIONSHIP WITH GOD!

Joretta K. Klepfer

Daily Choices

You may think there is no rhyme or reason to this book.
You may think it to be of strange order,
But no stranger than life itself.

For who among us knows the next day and its trials
    Or the next day and its joys?

Each day comes to us one at a time.

It is our choice to live it as we will
    Or as God wills.

It is our choice to face it with fear and trepidation
    Or with peace and joy.

It is our choice to struggle through it on our own
    Or place it in God's hands.

As you turn each page, you will find a piece of life.
If the mood matches your day, stay awhile and reflect.

If not, move on.
The next one may speak to you more.

More than anything, let God speak to you in some way,
    every day!

Just Pray!

I keep asking that the God of our Lord Jesus Christ, the glorious Father, may give you the Spirit of wisdom and revelation, so that you may know him better. I pray also that the eyes of your heart may be enlightened in order that you may know the hope to which he has called you, the riches of his glorious inheritance in the saints, and his incomparably great power for us who believe.

Ephesians 1:17-19a

JUST PRAY
    and enjoy a special relationship with God.

"Good morning, Lord"—
A simple beginning to the day with profound results.

What more does God ask of us than to be in relationship
    with him,
    and prayer is the foundation of that relationship.

The more time we spend in prayer,
    the stronger the relationship becomes.

The beautiful truth is that our prayers need not be
    complex, complicated or comprehensive,
    just honest and heartfelt.

Just begin the day with "Good morning, Lord."
    and revel in the joy of his presence.

Just tell him about your love for him
    and bask in the warmth of his love.

Joretta K. Klepfer

Just thank him for your life—all of it,
> the satisfactions and the sadness,
> the concerns and the celebrations.

Just hand your burdens over to him
> and he will heft them to his shoulders
> while he lifts the weight from yours.

Just rest in the wonder of his peace.

JUST PRAY!

Just Pray!

Show me your ways, O Lord,
teach me your paths;
guide me in your truth and teach me,
for you are God, my Savior,
and my hope is in you all day long.
Psalm 25:4-5

New Directions

The path I take
    I know not.

The future ahead
    I know not.

The hand I hold
    leads strong and sure.

It matters not
    that I know not!

Joretta K. Klepfer

Each one should use whatever gift he has received to serve others, faithfully administering God's grace in its various forms.
1 Peter 4:10

Fill me up, Lord!

Fill me to *ever*-flowing—
a constant stream of
>> your love,
>> your patience,
>> your tolerance,
>> your kindness,
>> your peace,
>> your joy

from you through me
to all who need
> a helping hand,
> a kind word,
> a listening heart.

Fill me up, Lord!

Just Pray!

In the past God spoke to our forefathers through the prophets at many times and in various ways, but in these last days he has spoken to us by his Son, whom he appointed heir of all things, and through whom he made the universe.

Hebrews 1:1-2

I Found You

Lord Jesus Christ,

> I found you yesterday
> > as I read your Word.
>
> I found you yesterday
> > in a cat's paw on my cheek.
>
> I found you yesterday
> > in clouds bringing life-giving rain.
>
> I found you yesterday
> > in a nest of baby birds.
>
> I found you yesterday
> > in a hug from a friend.
>
> I found you yesterday
> > in ... oh, so many ways.

Lord Jesus Christ,
> Open my eyes and my heart
> > to the ways I will find you today.

Joretta K. Klepfer

Set a guard over my mouth, O Lord;
    keep watch over the door of my lips.
Let not my heart be drawn to what is evil ...
                                                Psalm 141:3–4a

Forgive me, Lord,
    when I mistake my voice
    for yours.

From David's prayer:

I know, my God, that you test the heart and are pleased with integrity. All these things have I given willingly and with honest intent.

1 Chronicles 29:17a

Lead Me, Lord

Not my will, Lord, but yours
        is the test for my heart today.

Not my honor, Lord, but yours
        is the test for my words today.

Not my glory, Lord, but yours
        is the test for my actions today.

Not my path, Lord, but yours
        is the test for my life today.

Joretta K. Klepfer

I will praise you, O Lord, with all my heart;
I will tell of your wonders.
                                            Psalm 9:1

Good Morning, Lord.

What a way to start the day.

Watching the sunrise,
Hearing the birds say,
    "Come on, squirrels, get up and play."

Listening to the frantic chatter,
    wondering what could possibly be the
    matter on such a glorious day!

The cat perched on the fence is watching,
    now stalking.

No wonder the smaller ones are talking.
Actually they are laughing,
    knowing the game the fat cats play;
    knowing they can always scamper away.

What fun!
Simply the best way to start the day

Just Pray!

In the beginning God created the heavens and the earth.
Genesis 1:1

God's Art

Babes asleep;
    Kittens soft;
Blue eyes deep;
    Eagles aloft.

Mountains soaring;
    Salt flat plain;
Oceans roaring;
    Gentle rain.

Rainbow leaves;
    Rocks of gray;
Golden sheaves;
    Faithful May.

All combined
    Are simply dross.
His greatest work,
    An empty cross!

Joretta K. Klepfer

You are my lamp, O Lord; the Lord turns my darkness into light.
2 Samuel 22:29

And God said ...
    Let there be light.

And it is so!
    Every morning!

First a hint of orange glows in the deep blue at the horizon.

Then the sky moves imperceptibly through a
    beautiful rainbow of color.

The world becomes once again bathed in light,
    God's Light.

Even on cloudy days when the pale palette
    yields only brief shades of pink and blue
    before the gray,
His hand is unmistakable.

He will do the
    same wonderful miracle in our hearts!

Just Pray!

Then Jesus said to his disciples, "If anyone would come after me, he must deny himself and take up his cross and follow me. For whoever wants to save his life will lose it, but whoever loses his life for me will find it.

Matthew 16:24-25

Use me, Lord.

Open my heart to love,
Open my life to serve.

When I hear a small child in pain,
When I see homeless lives in rain,
When I find broken hearts in despair,
When I hear cries of "No fair!"

Use me, Lord.

Open my heart to love,
Open my life to serve.

When all around me is littered with trash,
When all I can breathe is pollution and ash,
When ribbons of concrete and asphalt take over,
When buildings abound where once was clover,

Use me, Lord.

Open my heart to love,
Open my life to serve.

Joretta K. Klepfer

When grief threatens to overwhelm,
When anger becomes too strong to calm,
When deceit tears relationships apart,
When worry, anxiety break open a heart,

        Use me, Lord.

Open my heart to love,
Open my life to serve.

Just Pray!

"If you love me, you will obey what I command. and I will ask the Father, and he will give you another Counselor to be with you forever—the Spirit of truth ... I will not leave you as orphans; I will come to you."

John 14:15-17a, 18

Lord come to me

Lord come to me
    wherever I roam
    and lead me home.

Lord come to me
    in dark of night,
    in daylight bright.

Lord come to me
    in times of stress
    when I'm a mess.

Lord come to me
    when joy abounds,
    with love surround.

Lord come to me!!

Joretta K. Klepfer

Moses speaks to Joshua:

The Lord himself goes before you and will be with you; he will never leave you nor forsake you. Do not be afraid; do not be discouraged.

Deuteronomy 31:8

Go with me today, Lord.

Help me find you in all places.

Help me meet you in all faces.

Help me see you in all races.

Help me eliminate all traces
   of bitterness,
        hopelessness
               and despair.

Go with me today, Lord.

Just Pray!

Though I sit in darkness, the Lord will be my light.
Micah 7:8b

I forgot to light our candle, Lord,
    but no matter.

The darkness surrounds me, Lord,
    but no matter.

The heart has light that knows no end.

The heart has light only you can send—
    the light of love, of joy, of peace.

The heart has light that will not cease.

A light so bright I lose myself,
    but no matter!

Joretta K. Klepfer

Search me, O God, and know my heart;
*   test me and know my anxious thoughts.*
See if there is any offensive way in me,
*   and lead me in the way everlasting.*
*   Psalm 139:23-24*

Lord, I need your gift of listening today,
    of listening to you through others' voices.

Lord, I need your gift of discernment today,
    of knowing the path you would have me take.

Lord, I need your gift of faith today,
    of faith in your voice,
    of faith in following the path where you lead.

Lord, I praise you today for your steadfast presence within me.

Lord, I thank you today
    for your love which never leaves me,
    for your peace which steadies me,
    for the joy of being with you in Christ.

Amen

Just Pray!

I am still confident of this:
    I will see the goodness of the Lord
    in the land of the living.
Wait for the Lord;
    be strong, and take heart,
    and wait for the Lord.
                                  Psalm 27:13-14

Throughout my days
    I shall wait for the Lord.
With patient ways
    I shall wait for the Lord.
With outstretched hands
    I shall wait for the Lord.
For kingdom plans
    I shall wait for the Lord.

Joretta K. Klepfer

Trust in the Lord with all your heart
and lean not on your own understanding.
Proverbs 3:5

I only know THAT and WHAT,
    HOW and WHY doesn't matter.
That God loves me so much is all I need.
    I don't have to understand the mystery.

Just Pray!

My purpose is that they may be encouraged in heart and united in love, so that they may know the mystery of God, namely Christ, in whom are hidden all the treasures of wisdom and knowledge.

Colossians 2:2-3

How vs. That

How is not nearly so important as *that!*

How God created the world is trivial.
That he did is awesome!

How God became man means little.
That he did means everything!

How God lives within us matters not.
That he does is peace and joy.

How God loves us so much (us, the unlovable)
        passes all understanding.
That he does is an incredible knowing of the heart.

How Jesus saved us by dying in our place
        is not nearly as important as *that* he did.

How we respond to God's love
        is not nearly as important as *that* we do
by caring,
    loving,
        serving!

Joretta K. Klepfer

Teach me your way, O Lord,
*   and I will walk in your truth;*
give me an undivided heart,
*   that I may fear your name.*
*   Psalm 86:11*

Meet me at sunrise, Lord.

    Show me your way.

Open my mind to that which confounds me.

Open my eyes to the beauty around me.

 Open my heart to your pleading.

Open my life to your leading.

Meet me at sunrise, Lord.

    Let's plan our day.

Just Pray!

Come to me all you who are weary and burdened and I will give you rest. Take my yoke upon you and learn from me, for I am gentle and humble in heart and you will find rest for your souls.
Matthew 11:28-29

Lord Jesus Christ,
You carried the heavy load of the cross for us
And now we can find rest in you because you still
      carry the load for us.
You give us a peace deeper than human understanding.
You give us a joy greater than our own making.
You give us rest blessed with your immeasurable love.
Thank you.

Joretta K. Klepfer

My sheep listen to my voice; I know them, and they follow me. I give them eternal life and they shall never perish; no one can snatch them out of my hand.

John 10:26

Lord, you spoke to me and said,

    "Rest here. Watch and listen."

But I went on.

Lord, you spoke to me and said,
    "Walk here. The place is serene.
    The way is quiet."

But I went on.

My quest was for a personal gain,
    but the walk to no avail.
The object was gone.

I turned back.

This time to walk through the wood serene,
    to discover the moss so green,
    and the unknown vine with red berries.

And I went on.

Just Pray!

This time to pause on the bench
    and hear your words,
        to write from my heart,
            to be not apart
              from your voice.

And we go on
Together.

Joretta K. Klepfer

And even the very hairs of your head are all numbered.
Matthew 10:30

Green is an unusual color for a rock.

Size doesn't matter if you're green—
you can still be seen!

You can tumble around
and still be found.

God knows where each tiny stone is
because each tiny stone is HIS

and so am I!

Just Pray!

... let your light shine before men that they may see your good works and praise your father in Heaven.
Matthew 5:16

Show us the way, Lord.

Your light is streaming through bare trees,
Birds chatter, squirrels scatter,

> The world wakes up.

Your light is streaming through bare hearts;
You choose us, you use us,

> The world wakes up.

Show us the way, Lord,

> To be your love, your hands
> reaching out
>   lifting up.

Joretta K. Klepfer

There are different kinds of service, but the same Lord.
1 Corinthians 12:5

Just Pray, "What's Next, Lord?"

Put your life in God's hands and see his miracles come forth.
Let him use your hands to serve manna to the hungry.
Let him use your eyes to read to the blind.
Let him use your ears to hear the voice of despair.
Let him use your legs to lift beams of injustice off the
　　backs of the oppressed.
Let him use your pen to the share the joys of his Word.
Let him use your heart to share the peace of his mercy.

Just Pray!

May God himself, the God of peace, sanctify you through and through. May your whole spirit, soul and body be kept blameless at the coming of our Lord Jesus Christ. The one who calls you is faithful and he will do it.
1 Thessalonians 5:23-24

Lord, be with me today.
    Touch my life in all I do.
    Touch my life in all I say.
    Touch my life in every way.
Lord, be with me today.

Joretta K. Klepfer

Therefore I tell you, do not worry about your life, what you will eat or drink; or about your body, what you will wear ... But seek first his kingdom and his righteousness, and all these things will be given to you as well.
Matthew 6:25a, 33

Am I in denial, Lord?
    or is it simply trust?
Is the reality mine or yours?
Help me make your reality mine.

You said not to worry, so I don't.
You said you will take care of my needs
    and you have
    and you will.
You said you would send your Spirit
    to stay with me
    and so I have peace.

Just Pray!

This is the day the Lord has made,
 let us rejoice and be glad in it.
  Psalm 118:24

Each day is yours, Lord.
 Lead me.

Each day I find you in a different place.
Each day I see you in a different face.

 Lead me, Lord.

Where today, Lord?
What serves you best?

Be my strength.
Be my guide.
Be my light in the darkness.

Lead me, Lord.

Do not let your hearts be troubled. Trust in God, trust also in me ... I am the way, the truth and the life. No one comes to the Father except through me.

John 14:1, 6

Jesus says, "I AM HE."

Are you searching for someone to care for you?
    Jesus says, "I AM HE."
Are you searching for someone to love you no matter what?
    Jesus says, "I AM HE."
Are you searching for a friend?
    Jesus says, "I AM HE."
Are you seeking forgiveness?
    Jesus says, "LOOK TO ME."
Are you searching for a path and purpose to your life?
    Jesus says, "FOLLOW ME."

Just Pray!

Who can discern his errors?
 Forgive my hidden faults.
Keep your servant also from willful sins;
 may they not rule over me.
                               Psalm 19:12-13a

Lord, forgive me
 for being less than you want me to be,
 for focusing more on what I want me to be.

Lord, forgive me
 for wanting to blame someone else
  for my shortcomings,
 for seeing only the faults of others
  and not my own.

Lord, forgive me
 for selfish thoughts,
 for thoughtless deeds,
 for unmet promises.

Joretta K. Klepfer

You are God my stronghold.
Send forth your light and your truth,
let them guide me;
Psalm 43:2a, 3a

Lord, be in my work today.

    Guide me while I play.

Lord, be in my life today.

    Help me find your way.

Just Pray!

Humble yourselves, therefore, under God's mighty hand, that he may lift you up in due time. Cast all your anxiety on him because he cares for you.

1 Peter 5:6-7

If you pray, then how can you worry?
Your concerns and worries are in God's hands
      and his will, WILL be done.
If his answer comes right away, be glad.
If his answer comes in recognizable form, be glad.
God knows what is best for us—
      what we need,
      when we need it.
God's time is not always ours
      but he will give us patience.
God's will is not always our choice for our lives
      but acceptance will bring us peace.

Joretta K. Klepfer

Praise the Lord all you nations;
    extol him, all you peoples.
For great is his love toward us,
    and the faithfulness of the Lord
    endures forever.

Psalm 117:1-2a

You're always there, Lord—
    Bringing me back to you;
    Keeping me close;
    Soothing my hurts;
    Celebrating my joys;
    Protecting me from harm;
    Meeting my needs;
    Forgiving my sins.

Thank you.

Just Pray!

He has showed you, O man, what is good.
And what does the Lord require of you?
To act justly and to love mercy
and to walk humbly with your God.
                                    Micah 6:8

Who me, Lord?

Who are you calling me to be?
What are you calling me to do?
How do I serve you best?

Questions for now,
        questions for later,
                questions for every day.

Keep me alert, Lord,
        ever ready to follow your will for my life.

Joretta K. Klepfer

For God did not give us a spirit of timidity, but a spirit of power, of love and self-discipline.
2 Timothy 1:7

Lord, please help me stay focused
    on your Word,
        not my work.

Lord, please help me stay focused
    on your message,
        not my mess.

Lord, please help me stay focused
    on reaching out in your name,
        not my own.

Just Pray!

"If I go and prepare a place for you, I will come back and take you to be with me that you also may be where I am."
                                                                John 14:3

Go ahead of me, Jesus.
Be in my dreams before my sleeping.
Be in my awareness before my waking.

Go ahead of me, Jesus.
Be in each thought before I think it.
Be in each word before I say it.

Go ahead of me, Jesus.
Be in each step before I take it.
Be in each room before I enter it.

"Show me your ways, O Lord;
Teach me your paths."

Words of old from David
        transferred to your servant of now.

Joretta K. Klepfer

Show me the way I should go,
for to you I lift up my soul.

Psalm 143:7

You act first, Lord.
You lead the way.
I can let go of my need to control
    since you are in charge.
I can quit worrying about mundane matters
    and just focus on you.
Lead me where you want me to go.
Show me what you want me to do—
    not just in the distant future
    but today
    right here
    right now
Each step I take, make it yours.

Just Pray!

God did this so that men would seek him and find him, though he perhaps is not far from each one of us. For in him we live and move and have our being."

Acts 17:27-28a

Keep me close, Lord.
Pull me back to you when I run away.
Help me find your place for me.
Help me find my place in you.
In all my ways
        for all my days
Help me be in you.

Joretta K. Klepfer

Surely God is my salvation;
I will trust and not be afraid.

                                          Isaiah 12:2a

Lord, I've been letting my doubt get in your way.
Teach me to trust you more.

Lord, I've been letting my fear get in your way.
Teach me to trust you more.

Lord, I've been letting my anxiety get in your way.
Teach me to trust you more.

Help me live my faith in you
       and not just talk about it.

Help me destroy the wall I have built between us.
Help me fling open the door to my life, my heart
       and live with the complete joy and abandonment
       of life with you in charge.

Just Pray!

For you created my inmost being;
 you knit me together in my mother's womb.
I praise you because I am fearfully and wonderfully made;
 your works are wonderful,
 I know that full well.
                              Psalm 139:13-14

Christ is the master quilter.
He pulls the various pieces of our lives together
 to create a work of art.

Pieces that have no real significance alone become,
 in concert with one another,
  a beautiful whole with meaning and purpose.

Joretta K. Klepfer

But now that you have been set free from sin and have become slaves to God, the benefit you reap leads to holiness, and the result is eternal life. For the wages of sin is death, but the gift of God is eternal life in Christ Jesus our Lord.
Romans 6:22-23

Lord Jesus Christ,
    Come be with me.

Lord Jesus Christ,
    Come set me free
    from this world of self.

Lord Jesus Christ,
    Come lead me to you each day.

Lord Jesus Christ,
    Come be my guide to walk
    the path you choose.

Lord Jesus Christ,
    Come be with me.

Just Pray!

For the foolishness of God is wiser than man's wisdom and the weakness of God is stronger than man's strength.
1 Corinthians 1:25

Lord, my need for your love is great
    but not greater than your capacity to provide;
    not greater than your generosity and compassion.

Lord, my need for your mercy is great
    but not greater than your willingness to forgive.

Lord, my need for your Word is great
    but not greater than your patience
    with my slow steps in learning;

Lord, my need for your grace is great
    but not greater than your loving faithfulness
    in drawing me close to you when I stray.

Joretta K. Klepfer

For God, who said, "Let light shine out of darkness," made his light shine in our hearts to give us the light of the knowledge of the glory of God in the face of Christ.
1 Corinthians 4:6

Keep your light burning in my heart, Lord.

> Though the day is gray with worry;
> Though the night is dark with sorrow;
> Knowing you are always with me,
> I keep faith in your tomorrow.

Keep your light burning in my heart, Lord.

Day after day, in the temple courts and from house to house, they never stopped teaching and proclaiming the good news that Jesus is the Christ.
Acts 5:42

Christians Don't Retire!

Lord Jesus Christ,
Keep my feet ever set on your path.
Keep my heart freely fixed on serving you.
Keep my mind ever alert to hearing
    and learning your Word.

Joretta K. Klepfer

So do not fear, for I am with you;
　do not be dismayed, for I am your God.
I will strengthen you and help you;
　I will uphold you with my righteous right hand.
　　　　　　　　　　　　　　Isaiah 41:10

Lord Jesus Christ,
　Come be with me.
　Come take me by the hand
　　　and show me what you would have me see.
　Come push me from behind to those places
　　　where I am reluctant to go,
　　　but where you need me to be.
　Come lift me up with your loving hands
　　　when I can't do that for myself.

Just Pray!

He is a shield
 for all who take refuge in him.
It is God who arms me with strength
 and makes my way perfect.
                               Psalm 18:30b, 32

Thank you, Lord.
Thank you for the joy
 and helping me live through the pain.
Thank you for the shafts of sun
 and life-giving drops of rain.

My life is in your hands, Lord.
Use me in your plans, Lord.
I'm just one grain of sand, Lord.

Still, I know that
 you know
 who and where I am.

Thank you, Lord.

Joretta K. Klepfer

Look at the birds of the air; they do not sow or reap or store away in barns, and yet your heavenly Father feeds them. Are you not more valuable than they?
Matthew 6:26

The constant rustle of the leaves
Made me turn first left
Then right
Again and again
Until the motion of the small birds caught my eye,
Dozens of them pecking away
At unseen treasures beneath the leaves.

God provides a feast for them.
Surely he will send manna for me.

Just Pray!

I tell you the truth, if you have faith as small as a mustard seed, you can say to this mountain, 'Move from here to there' and it will move. Nothing will be impossible for you.
Matthew 17:20-21

Need help?

If you catch yourself thinking, "I can't"
    Stop!
    Say aloud, "I can."

If you catch yourself saying, "I won't"
    Stop!
    Say aloud, "I will."

If you catch yourself trying to solve your own problems,
    Stop!
    Say aloud, "You and me, Lord.
        Together we can move mountains,
        Maybe all at once,
        Maybe one stone at a time.
        Maybe speed doesn't matter
            as long as we're together.
    You and me, Lord."

Joretta K. Klepfer

I desire to do your will, O my God;
  your law is within my heart.
Do not withhold your mercy from me, O Lord;
  may your love and truth always protect me.
      Psalm 40:8, 11 (of David)

Lord, be with me, for it is morning—
  there is much to do today;
  there are many words to say—your words;
  there is much love to share—your love;
  there are many hugs and smiles to give;
  there are many people to bring to you.

Lord, be with me, for it is evening—
  time to remember the joys of the day;
  time to quiet the worries and give them to you;
  time to find your balm to soothe harried
      nerves and stormy relationships;
  time to rest in your peace.

Lord, be with me.

Just Pray!

A new command I give you: Love one another. As I have loved you, so you must love one another. By this all men will know you are my disciples, if you love one another.
John 13:34

Open my eyes, Lord.

Help me see what you see—
    the despair of poverty,
    the pain of hunger,
    the sorrow of death,
    the disappointment of
        lost jobs,
        lost dreams,
        lost relationships.

Open my heart, Lord.

Help me feel your presence
    walking beside me,
    working through me
    to be your hands and heart
    reaching out with your love.

Joretta K. Klepfer

You have made known to me the path of life; you will fill me with joy in your presence, with eternal pleasures at your right hand.

Psalm 16:11

Good morning, Lord.

What shall we do today?
Be in my head,
Be in my heart
Through all my work and play.

Just Pray!

Out of the depths I cry to you, O Lord.
  O Lord, hear my voice.
I wait for the Lord, my soul waits,
  and in his word I put my hope.
                              Psalm 130:1, 5

Dear Heavenly Father,
Gracious, loving, merciful
  I praise you.
Forgiving, faithful, steadfast
  I praise you.
For my lack of serving others,
  Forgive me and help me to change.
For my lack of diligent study of your Word,
  Forgive me and help me to change.
For my lack of inviting others to know you,
  Forgive me and help me to change.
For love and laughter,
  faith and forgiveness,
  life and liberty,
  family and friends,
  bountiful blessings,
Thank you!

Joretta K. Klepfer

*Your word is a lamp to my feet
and a light for my path*
Psalm 119:105

Keep me focused on you, Lord

Make clear the pathway ahead.
    Direct the steps that I take.
Open the door to your will.
    Guide each decision I make.

Keep me focused on you, Lord.

When Jesus spoke again to the people, he said "I am the light of the world. Whoever follows me will never walk in darkness but will have the light of life."

John 8:12

Help me, Lord.
I try to remember what you said, but
    sometimes the darkness overwhelms me.
What a comfort to know your light is always shining.
What a comfort to see your light ahead of me,
    leading the way to you.
What a comfort to find your loving hand reaching for me.
What a comfort to bask in the warm light of your love
    surrounding me.
Help me stay in your light, Lord.

Joretta K. Klepfer

Be completely humble and gentle; be patient, bearing with one another in love. Make every effort to keep the unity of the Spirit through the bond of peace.

Ephesians 4:2-3

Lord Jesus Christ,
    Your Word guides my path;
        Help me share your light.

    Your light renews my heart;
        Help me share your love.

    Your love heals my spirit;
        Help me share your peace.

    Your peace gives rest to my soul;
        Help me share your joy.

Just Pray!

Be self-controlled and alert. Your enemy the devil prowls around like a roaring lion looking for someone to devour. Resist him, standing firm in the faith ...

1 Peter 5:8-9a

Am I just chaff, Lord,
      or do I have the substance of grain?
Does my faith blow away at the slightest hint of doubt,
      or does it stand fast through the winds of change,
          trusting your plans for me?
You know best, Lord.
Help me to be open to your direction, your path,
      for my life.

Joretta K. Klepfer

The Lord is my rock, my fortress and my deliverer;
He is a shield for all who take refuge in him.
                                              Psalm 18:2a, 30b

It's cold today.

    Wrap me in your arms, Lord.
        Keep me safe and warm.

        The world outside is cold and gray.
        The people there have lost their way.

    Wrap me in your arms, Lord.
        Keep the world at bay.

Forgive my self-centeredness and remind me, Lord—

To be with you, to follow you,
    is to lose me.

To follow you is to step out of the boat;
To follow you is to climb out on that limb;
To follow you is to walk away from the crowd.

To follow you means
    to look for you down every street,
    to share your love with all I meet,
    to spend time just sitting at your feet.

To follow you means
    sometimes to risk all,
    always to gain all.

To follow you means life
    always and forever,
    wrapped in your arms,
    safe and warm
Even when it's cold outside.

Just Pray!

Be joyful always; pray continually; give thanks in all circumstances, for this is God's will for you in Christ Jesus.
1 Thessalonians 5:16-18

Make ALL-YEAR resolutions!

Resolve each day to
>Pray,
>Love God and others,
>Find joy wherever you are,
>Be at peace in your heart,
>Tell someone about Jesus.

Joretta K. Klepfer

And being found in appearance as a man,
he humbled himself
and became obedient to death—
even death on a cross!

Philippians 2:8

Let's have a "come to Jesus" meeting.
Let me tell you about our Lord.

About his love ...
>He gave us all he had to give—his life!
>And he triumphed!
>He reached out to all people
>>And he counts on us to do the same.
>
>His love is obvious in the creation he gave us.
>>How glorious are his works!

About his grace ...
>He gave himself as the final sacrifice for our sins.
>He died that our sins will be forgiven
>He died that we might have eternal life.
>He died that we might live with him forever.

About his peace ...
>He gave us—
>A peace like no other.
>A peace beyond our understanding
>>but not our experience.
>
>A peace deep in our hearts when we accept him
>>and live in his presence.

Just Pray!

About his joy ...
>We can find joy in all circumstances because
>we are claimed as his.
>Joy is not man-made;
>>it is Jesus' gift to us.

Joretta K. Klepfer

May the words of my mouth and the
meditation of my heart
be pleasing in your sight,
O Lord, my Rock, and my Redeemer.
Psalm 19:14

Lord Jesus Christ,
As I go about my work this day—
    Let your thoughts be in my head.
    Let your words be on my lips.
    Let your love be in my heart.
    Let your path be the guide for my feet.
    Let me live my life ever aware of your presence.

Just Pray!

> *Enter his gates with thanksgiving*
> *and his courts with praise;*
> *give thanks to him and praise his name.*
> *Psalm 100:4*

Your blessings are many, Lord.
    My responses too few.
Open my eyes.
    Jolt me out of my comfortable world.
    Jar me from my complacency.
    Push me into awareness of the needs of your people.
    Pull me into the mainstream of need and suffering.
Direct my days
    to see the ways
        I can serve you with praise
            and thanksgiving.

Joretta K. Klepfer

May our Lord Jesus Christ himself and God our Father, who loved us and by his grace gave us eternal encouragement and good hope, encourage your hearts and strengthen you in every good deed and word.
2 Thessalonians 2:16-17

Am I a tourist or pilgrim?
What is God asking me to leave behind?
What grace do I need to seek as I go on?

Questions to ponder ...

>as I set out with camera in hand—a tourist tool—
>to record for all, the flowers, the birds,
>the mountains, this land!

>The elusive woodpecker sounds his laughter
>>between the rat-a-tat of his iron beak,
>darting to and fro among the trees,
>daring the lens to get a peek.

So easy
    the
        downward
            glide
                for
                    winter muscles
                          little used.

So easy the wayward slide for the mind,
    leaving the questions never mused.

Just Pray!

Then the path changes.

The solitude suddenly seems menacing.
I feel alone and vulnerable.
The hill is steep.
My breath comes heavy.
I feel the outer cold.

But I sense an inner warmth

I begin to pray:
With inward breath, "Lord Jesus Christ"
With breath expelled, "Be with me today."

Then the way grows shorter.
The steepness planes.
My strength returns with each step.

I reach the top with soaring spirit.

The tourist becomes pilgrim!

And what have I learned?
The tourist takes a journey of the senses.
The pilgrim takes a journey of the heart.

Joretta K. Klepfer

And I will do whatever you ask in my name, so that the Son may bring glory to the Father. You may ask me for anything in my name, and I will do it.

John 14:13-14

Lord Jesus Christ,
    Be with me today.
Lord Jesus Christ,
    Teach me to pray,
      "Lord Jesus Christ."

Let all I do
    Be a prayer to you.

Just Pray!

For in him you have been enriched in every way—in all your speaking and in all your knowledge—because our testimony about Christ was confirmed in you. Therefore you do not lack any spiritual gift as you wait for our Lord Jesus Christ to be revealed.

1 Corinthians 1:5-7

Lord, have I let your light dim in my heart?
    Forgive me.
Lord, have I let other voices be louder than yours?
    Forgive me.
Lord, have I put you last in my life?
    Forgive me.
For strength to find you again,
    Help me, Lord.
For courage to put you first in all my life,
    Bless me, Lord.
For your love, which permeates my total being,
    Thank you, Lord.
For your peace, which surrounds me,
    Thank you, Lord.
For your Spirit, which lives in my heart,
    Thank you, Lord.

Joretta K. Klepfer

The Lord gives strength to his people;
the Lord blesses his people with peace.
Psalm 29:11

Direct my days, Lord,
    that I may work through you.

Give peace to my nights
    that I may rest in you.

Just Pray!

Jesus answered, "I tell you the truth, no one can enter the kingdom of God unless he is born of water and the Spirit. Flesh gives birth to flesh, but the Spirit gives birth to spirit.
John 3:5-6

The question to ponder—
    Where/what are your sacred places?

For me
"A sacred place" is scattered over 55 years;
    a campfire worship at a mountaintop retreat,
    a candlelight worship under the stars,
    a sunset worship by the ocean.

But the first real Christ relationship
    began on Mother's Day
    at youth retreat worship, 1972.

IT WAS RAINING!!

I could say it was raining cats and dogs
    but it was really the pure water of a
    renewed baptism in Christ.

What about you?

Joretta K. Klepfer

I was filled with delight day after day,
*   rejoicing always in his presence,*
rejoicing in his whole world
*   and delighting in mankind.*

Proverbs 8:30b-31

Delight

Take delight in the sun and moon and stars.
Take delight in the Son and Creator and Spirit.

Take delight in light things.
Take delight in bright things.

Take delight in gray things.
Take delight in rainbow things.

Take delight in big things.
Take delight in small things.

Take delight in ALL things.

Take delight, please.

Just Pray!

*The earth is the Lord's, and everything in it,
the world, and all who live in it;*

Psalm 24:1

The earth,
    The rocks,
        The green moss amongst the gray—

God's forever.

We are
    Living,
        Breathing,
            Loving,
                Serving—

God's forever.

Joretta K. Klepfer

Finally, be strong in the Lord and in his mighty power. Put on the full armor of God so that you can take your stand against the devil's schemes. For our struggle is not against flesh and blood, but against the rulers, against the authorities, against the powers of this dark world and against the spiritual forces of evil in the heavenly realms

Ephesians 6:10-12

Old habits, Lord!

Old habits creep in between   us.

So easy to slip back into the old me   away from you.

Keep me diligent, ever alert to the devious ways of the evil one.

One small
    slip today,   a wider gap tomorrow.

What a comfort to know you are ever vigilant,
always loving, bringing me back to you.

Just Pray!

"Peace I leave with you; my peace I give you."
John 14:27

Lord Jesus Christ,
Be with me this day.
Guide me through each piece of it.
Help me find your peace in it.
Help me find your way.

Joretta K. Klepfer

Here I am! I stand at the door and knock. If anyone hears my voice and opens the door, I will come in and eat with him, and he with me.
Revelation 3:20

You are my center, Lord.

How do I know where to go?
How do I see where to be?

You are my center, Lord.

Your presence real; your love I feel.
Your gift of peace makes all doubts cease.

You are my center, Lord.

You knock at the door, saying
"Just open, nothing more."

You lift me up; you fill my cup
With blessings

You are my center, Lord.

Just Pray!

In the morning, O Lord, you hear my voice;
in the morning I lay my requests before you
and wait in expectation.
                                        Psalm 5:3

Listen to the sounds of your world, Lord.

    Joy abounds.

Listen to the squirrels chatter as they scatter
    tree to tree not stopping to rest;

    to the birds calling young ones
    from the nest;

    to the dog barking at the cat
    perched on the fence above.

Then hear the low moaning sound of the
    mourning dove.

The peaceful dawn gives way
    to Monday's frantic pace.

Thanks for the brief time with you
    in this special place.

Joretta K. Klepfer

If anyone says, "I love God," yet hates his brother, he is a liar. For anyone who does not love his brother, whom he has seen, cannot love God, whom he has not seen.

1 John 4:20

Lord, in your love,

> we can show love.

Lord, in your mercy,

> we can be forgiving.

Lord, in your love

> we can care and share.

Lord, in your mercy

> we can find peace.

Just Pray!

... let your light shine before men, that they may see your good deeds and praise your Father in heaven.
Matthew 5:16

The Vase

The vase can hold flowers
        but a candle is better.

The vase is wondrously made—
        ruffled edge,
        concave and convex,
        round and oval
        pieces of glass,
All to portray the light within through its many facets.

The light of Christ shines brightly,
        but diffusely,
        reflected all around,
Just like His light within us.

Though we can't see the source of the flame,
        we can see its effects.

We can glow with His light!

Joretta K. Klepfer

Do not be anxious about anything, but in everything, by prayer and petition, with thanksgiving, present your requests to God. And the peace of God, which transcends all understanding, will guard your hearts and your minds in Christ Jesus.
Philippians 4:6-7

The candle has limits, Lord,

    but you don't.

It's tallow burns up, Lord,

    but your fire is ever bright;

    your beam showing the way;

    your glow reflecting all around;

    your light of love never ceasing;

    your love in our hearts ever increasing

    with

    joy not contained,

    peace not explained,

    love not restrained,

    mystery sustained.

Just Pray!

But in your hearts set apart Christ as Lord. Always be prepared to give an answer to everyone who asks you to give the reason for the hope that you have.

1 Peter 3:15

The Call

First to find Christ in me

    So I can show Christ to you.

If you find Christ in me,

    Then you can find Christ in you.

If I find Christ in you,

    Then I can find Christ in me.

Joretta K. Klepfer

To the Jews who had believed him, Jesus said, "If you hold to my teaching, you are really my disciples. Then you will know the truth, and the truth will set you free."

John 8:31-32

Lord Jesus Christ,
    Be with me today;
        Teach me your way.

Lord Jesus Christ,
    Teach me to live;
        Teach me to give.

Lord Jesus Christ,
    Teach me to care;
        Teach me to share
            your love, your peace
            with all I meet.

Lord Jesus Christ,
    I sit at your feet.

Just Pray!

For he will command his angels concerning you
to guard you in all your ways;
they will lift you up in their hands,
so that you will not strike your foot against a stone.
Psalm 91:11-12

Why does the candle flicker
when the air is still all around?

But for the wings of angels standing guard nearby
watching, always watching, over me.

No wonder I have always felt blessed.

God's guardians are ever at their post.

Joretta K. Klepfer

Now the Lord is the Spirit, and where the Spirit of the Lord is, there is freedom.
2 Corinthians 3:17

Turn the dial of life, O Lord.

    Tune me in.

Find WGOD for me,

    So I can be With Good Old Dad.

Seek out WJCL

    So I can be With Jesus Christ Live.

Search for WHSN

    So I can be With Holy Spirit Now.

Thank you for the liberties, Lord,

    but keep me tuned into you.

Just Pray!

On the last and greatest day of the Feast, Jesus stood and said in a loud voice, "If anyone is thirsty, let him come to me and drink. Whoever believes in me, as the Scripture has said, streams of living water will flow from within him."

John 7:37-38

Distractions are all around me, Lord,

Voices louder than yours.

Tune my ears to hear you first.

Tune my heart to obey my thirst

    for the holy water of your Word.

Joretta K. Klepfer

You prepare a table before me
    in the presence of my enemies.
You anoint my head with oil;
    my cup overflows.

Psalm 23:5

I'm empty, Lord.

    Fill me up!

Just Pray!

If anyone acknowledges that Jesus is the Son of God, God lives in him and he in God. And so we know and rely on the love God has for us.

1 John 4:15-16

Lord, come to me.

Lord, come to me in the quiet of the night

    and in the busyness of the day.

Lord, come to me with your power and might.

    Dispel all fears, worries, and dismay.

Lord, come to me with joy, with peace, with love

    That I may treasure and share these gifts of the dove.

Lord, come to me in every way, with all your might

    in every day and every night.

Lord, come to me

Joretta K. Klepfer

"I have told you these things, so that in me you may have peace. In this world you will have trouble. But take heart! I have overcome the world."

John 16:33

Peace
        can come in the midst of a storm
        like the
        still calm
        in the eye of a hurricane.

Peace
        is not the same as still.

        Still can hide smoldering.
        Still can hide rot and mold.

Chaos can abound
        all around
        but

Peace from God centers us in its midst.

Peace of mind is really
        Peace of heart.

Peace means
        be not apart
                from God.

Just Pray!

"For God so loved the world that he gave his one and only Son, that whoever believes in him shall not perish but have eternal life.
John 3:16

Cancer is such a scary word.
    Where does it end, Lord?

Another one today.
Another one for my care list.
Another one for my prayer list.
Another one to bring to you.

This time a dear friend,
    before that an aunt,
        a cousin,
        a friend's mother-in-law,
        another dear friend,
        and another dear friend,
    long ago a father.

These beautiful ones fight valiantly;
    all I place in your hands;
    all in need of your healing touch,
        your love,
        your peace.

Give to all your gift of peace, which comes with
    surrender of our will to yours.

Joretta K. Klepfer

Give to all your gift of peace, which comes in saying
"Not mine, but your will be done."

Give to all your gift of peace, which comes in knowing
that through Christ the real war is won.

Just Pray!

This is love: not that we loved God, but that he loved us and sent his Son as an atoning sacrifice for our sins. Dear friends, since God so loved us, we also ought to love one another.
1 John 4:10-11

Faith

Family

Friends

What else really matters?

Joretta K. Klepfer

... In repentance and rest is your salvation,
in quietness and trust is your strength ...

Isaiah 30:15

The Quiet Way*

The Quiet Way beckons the soul.

The Quiet Way is not so quiet.

    The birds proclaim God's glory.

    The dead oak leaves chatter as they are coaxed to fall.

    The wind whistles through bare limbs.

    The bright red berries of an unknown vine shout "discover me!"

    The world awaits the resurrection with its winter voice.

* The Quiet Way is a meditation trail through the woods at Lutheridge, a Lutheran camping/conference center in the mountains of North Carolina.

Therefore, I urge you, brothers, in view of God's mercy, to offer your bodies as living sacrifices, holy and pleasing to God—this is your spiritual act of worship. Do not conform any longer to the pattern of this world, but be transformed by the renewing of your mind. Then you will be able to test and approve what God's will is—his good, pleasing and perfect will.

Romans 12:1-2

Change

God working within us.

God transforming,

God enlightening,

God re-forming,

God ever brightening

    our lives,

    our hearts

    with His love.

Joretta K. Klepfer

But we ought always to thank God for you, brothers loved by the Lord, because from the beginning God chose you to be saved through the sanctifying work of the Spirit and through belief in the truth. He called you to this through our gospel, that you might share in the glory of our Lord Jesus Christ.
2 Thessalonians 2:13-14

Create
    Redeem
        Sanctify

Mighty words, Lord

Create
    All that was
        All that is
            All that will be
                including me!
    Thank you, Lord

Redeem
    Buy back
        Recover
            Pay a premium
            at great price
                for me!
    Thank you, Lord

Sanctify
    Set apart as holy
        Consecrate
            Cleanse and set free
                Live within me.

    Thank you, Lord

Just Pray!

... the Spirit helps us in our weakness. We do not know what we ought to pray for, but the Spirit himself intercedes for us with groans that words cannot express ... And we know that in all things God works for the good of those who love him, who have been called according to his purpose.
Romans 8:26, 28

Lord, Be With Me.

Teach me what you would have me learn.

Show me what you would have me see.

Lead me where you would have me go.

Lord, Be With Me.

Speak to me what you would have me hear.

Surround me with the love you would have
me feel.

Settle me in the midst of chaos to sense
your peace.

Lord, Be With Me.

Help me live this day as
you would have me live it.

Joretta K. Klepfer

For you make me glad by your deeds, O Lord,
I sing for joy at the works of your hands.

Psalm 92:4

What joy, Lord!

A cat in the lap
        taking a nap.
Birds in the trees
        singing. A breeze
Cool on the face.
        This is my place!
The morning's glory proclaimed!
        The flower's aptly named.
Simple pleasures,
        Simple treasures
                to help me start my day.

Just Pray!

Now faith is being sure of what we hope for and certain of what we do not see.

Hebrews 11:1

Blind Faith

Blind to risk
        Open to challenge

Blind to doubt
        Open to understanding

Blind to hate
        Open to love

Joretta K. Klepfer

Yet the Lord longs to be gracious to you;
    he rises to show you compassion.
For the Lord is a God of justice.
    Blessed are all who wait for him!

                                                    Isaiah 30:18

How do I wait for the Lord?
Patiently sometimes,
      Impatiently other times;
With faith and anticipation;
With excitement and longing;
With faithfulness and dedication;
With passion!

Just Pray!

Heal me, O Lord, and I will be healed;
save me and I will be saved,
for you are the one I praise.

Jeremiah 17:14

Heal this body, Lord,
        that I may serve you better.

Heal this heart, Lord,
        that I may love you more.

Heal this mind, Lord,
        that I may know your ways.

Heal this soul, Lord,
        that your peace will be my peace.

Joretta K. Klepfer

Give thanks to the Lord, for he is good;
his love endures forever.
Psalm 107:1

Lord, make me aware
    that every movement in the day
    is a gift from you.

Lord, make me aware
    that every impulse to stop and play
    is a gift from you.

Lord, make me aware
    that each beautiful butterfly,
        fluttering by;
    that every beautiful bird
        soaring high in the sky
    is a gift from you.

Lord, make me aware
    that time to learn,
        time to contemplate,
    that time to work,
        time to recreate,
    is a gift from you.

Lord, make me aware
    that time to think,
        time to reflect,
    that time to be still,
        time to expect
            a miracle,
    is a gift from you.

Lord, make me aware of all your gifts,
    but most of all,
        make me grateful!

Just Pray!

How lovely is your dwelling place,
   O Lord Almighty!
My soul yearns, even faints,
   for the courts of the Lord;
my heart and my flesh cry out
   for the living God.
                                       Psalm 84:1-2

Here I am again, Lord.

Watching your sunrise,
   experiencing the wonder of your world
   and feeling blessed.

How much I take for granted!

How many times I look without really seeing!

Open my senses to
   —the simple beauty of your light
      streaming through the trees;

   —the birds' melodies drifting with the breeze;

   —the cool brisk feel to the morning as
      a taste of fall brings respite
      to the summer's heat.

Joretta K. Klepfer

May the God of hope fill you with all joy and peace as you trust in him, so that you may overflow with hope by the power of the Holy Spirit.

Romans 15:13

How Do You Say Good-bye?

My best friend is moving.

Far away.

Too far for an impromptu lunch.
Too far for an afternoon of shopping.
Too far for sharing fresh bread or homemade cookies.
Too far to rush over with chicken soup for healing.
Too far for a day trip to the mountains.

But with God all things are possible,
    So distances are surmountable.
Why else would we have been blessed with the technology
    for voice, fax, and e-mail,
        but to stay in touch with the ones we cherish?
Even old-fashioned delivery by eagle-express
    will serve us well
    but will not replace the presence—
        seeing the smile,
        feeling the hug,
            observing the silent language of the heart.
These memories I trust to God.

How do you say good-bye?
The same way you say hello ...

God be with you, my friend!

Just Pray!

The Lord is my strength and my shield;
    my heart trusts in him, and I am helped.
My heart leaps for joy
    and I will give thanks to him in song.
Psalm 28:7

Father God
    Creator of the universe
        and my small piece of it,

Thank you for
    sunshine and rain
    green grass
    tall trees
    colorful flowers
    bountiful creatures
    beautiful people.

All from your hand.
All show your touch.
All to be loved and appreciated
    much by me,
    more by you.

Lord Jesus Christ
    Savior of all people
    including me,

Thank you for
    living among us
    teaching us how to live
    showing us how to love
    bringing us peace
    dying horribly that we might live
        forever in your presence.

Joretta K. Klepfer

Holy Spirit
> Living presence
>> always in my heart

Thank you for
> your constant vigilance
> your unfailing patience with me
> your love surrounding me
> your peace which permeates my soul.

Thank you, Lord

Help me to remember to say the words
> that I feel in my heart!

Just Pray!

... those who hope in the Lord
*   will renew their strength.*
They will soar on wings like eagles;
*   they will run and not grow weary,*
*   they will walk and not be faint.*
*   Isaiah 40:31*

Today was tiring, Lord.
When I'm tempted to complain,
    remind me that my job really is easy.
When I feel frustrated at work,
    remind me that there are many without a job.
When I don't feel like cooking,
    remind me that there are many without food.
When I don't feel like cleaning,
    remind me that there are many without a home.
When I wish I could be doing something else,
    remind me that I can serve you wherever I am.

Joretta K. Klepfer

... we speak of God's secret wisdom, a wisdom that has been hidden and that God destined for our glory before time began. None of the rulers of this age understood it, for if they had, they would not have crucified the Lord of glory.
1 Corinthians 2:7-8

O Lord, you are my strength.
In your wisdom and time,
>Grant me courage to follow you.

In your wisdom and time,
>Grant me insight to determine the path
>you have chosen for me.

In your wisdom and time,
>Grant me patience to wait for your Word.

In your wisdom and time,
>Grant me discipline in staying focused
>on your work for me.

In your wisdom and time,
>Grant me faithfulness in serving you.

Just Pray!

Cleanse me with hyssop, and I will be clean;
wash me, and I will be whiter than snow.
Psalm 51:7

It snowed last night
   —a wonderful windless snow
        that left each flake to determine its
           own destiny;
   —a quiet snow
        to clean the world of chaos for one
           brief moment.
Today the wind comes
   cold and bitter,
   unrelenting and unforgiving,
   making the flakes fly again to unknown destinations.

Joretta K. Klepfer

I say to myself, "The Lord is my portion; therefore I will wait for him." The Lord is good to those whose hope is in him. It is good to wait quietly for the salvation of the Lord.
Lamentations 3:24-26

Speak, Lord, for your servant is listening.
Help me hear your word for me.
Help me distinguish your voice from all those
    who would lead me away from you.
Help me be patient and wait for your word, your time.
Your glory is great and your blessings are many.
I am grateful!

Just Pray!

Cast your cares on the Lord and he will sustain you.
Psalm 55:22

They are all yours, Lord.
I gladly give them to you
      —the worries
      —the headaches
      —the cares of everyday life
      —the future!
The peace you give is deep,
      more than I can understand
      but not more than I can enjoy.
I rest in your promises,
      your faithfulness,
      your love,
      your joy,
      your peace.

Joretta K. Klepfer

The angel said to the women, "Do not be afraid, for I know that you are looking for Jesus, who was crucified. He is not here; he has risen, just as he said. Come and see the place where he lay. Then go quickly and tell his disciples: 'He has risen from the dead and is going ahead of you into Galilee. There you will see him.'"

Matthew 28:5-7

Good Friday

Lord Jesus Christ
You died for me
  —to wipe away my sins.
  —to make me whole and pure in your sight.
  —to clothe me in your white cloak of righteousness.
  —to provide a way for me to gain eternal life.
  —to bring me peace and joy.
  —to show me love.
Thank you.

Saturday Vigil

It is cold and raining.
Somehow fitting as I reflect on your work
  this day so many years ago.
You died for me and conquered Satan.
You will still conquer Satan for me;
I have but to ask.

Easter Sunday

The world is cloudy
  The heart is bright.
Christ has conquered sin
  This holy night.

CHRIST IS RISEN!   ALLELUIA!

Just Pray!

You have made known to me the path of life;
you will fill me with joy in your presence,
with eternal pleasures at your right hand.
Psalm 16:11

Lord Jesus Christ,
    Fill my mind with your Word.
    Fill my heart with your love.
    Fill my soul with your peace.
    Fill my path with your purpose.
    Fill my life with your joy.
Lord Jesus Christ
    Fill me to overflowing!

Joretta K. Klepfer

But the fruit of the Spirit is love, joy, peace, patience, kindness, goodness, faithfulness, gentleness and self-control.
Galatians 5:22-23a

God is still creating.
    Let him create a new you, so that—
You toss away hate
    While he creates love.
You toss away brooding
    While he creates joy.
You toss away dissension
    While he creates peace.
You toss away anxiousness
    While he creates patience.
You toss away a mean spirit
    While he creates kindness.
You toss away evil thoughts
    While he creates goodness.
You toss away infidelity
    While he creates faithfulness.
You toss away anger
    While he creates gentleness.
You toss away self-centeredness
    While he creates self-control.

Just Pray!

> *Blessed are those who have learned to acclaim you,*
> *who walk in the light of your presence, O Lord.*
> *They rejoice in your name all day long;*
> *they exult in your righteousness.*
>
> *Psalm 89:15-16*

Make me aware, Lord.
    Your presence fills my every moment.
Make me aware, Lord.
    Your love fills my life in ways I can't comprehend.
    Your peace settles my heart when my life is
        filled with chaos.
Make me aware, Lord, that all of life and life itself
    is your gracious gift,
        freely given,
        dearly bought,
        lovingly provided.
I thank you.
Please know that I am thankful even when my
    sinful nature causes me to forget.
Please remind me to be aware and be thankful at those
    times when I get too busy with my own agenda.
Keep me on your path and keep me faithful to your Word.
Let all I do and say be pleasing to you.

Joretta K. Klepfer

Whenever the rainbow appears in the clouds, I will see it and remember the everlasting covenant between God and all living creatures of every kind on the earth.

Genesis 9:16

Spring

Suddenly the world is green again.
Just yesterday the first shoots of daffodils
      were peeking through dead leaves.
April is magic—
      all shades of pink, red,
      white, blue,
      purple, yellow and green.
God's rainbow on earth.
Another sign of his covenant.

Just Pray!

We wait in hope for the Lord;
 he is our help and our shield.
May your unfailing love rest upon us, O Lord,
 even as we put our hope in you.
Psalm 33:20, 22

Time slips by without notice—
    Unfocused life,
    Unpurposed life,
    Undriven life,
    Undisciplined life
But not without hope;
Hope that comes from faith in Jesus Christ.

Joretta K. Klepfer

Give ear to my words, O Lord,
consider my sighing.
Listen to my cry for help,
my King and my God,
for to you I pray.
In the morning, O Lord, you hear my voice,
in the morning I lay my requests before you
and wait in expectation.

Psalm 5:1-3

Wait.
It's hard, Lord,
But I do feel a sense of anticipation.
I know your timing is different from mine.
Forgive me for being impatient and wanting to rush
      into things.
Settle me down, Lord.
Help me to recognize your will for my life.
Help me to accept your will for my life.
Send me patience, Lord.
Help me be content to wait for your timing and
      your will to be done in my life.

Be still and know that I am God;
Psalm 46:10a

Practice the Prayer of Presence.

Just be still and sense the presence of God.
Just be still and feel his loving arms wrapped around you.
Just be still and rest in his peace.
Just be still and know you are forgiven.
Just be still and practice the prayer of presence.
Just be still.
Just be.

Joretta K. Klepfer

... let us be thankful, and so worship God acceptably with reverence and awe ...
Hebrews 12:28b

For the joy of gathering in your name,
For the joy of meeting you in old friends,
For the joy of discovering you through new friends,
THANK YOU, LORD.

For your love that we share in community, both close and far away,
For your love that we share with one another,
For your love that carries us through each day with a constant sense of your presence,
THANK YOU, LORD.

For your peace that comes from faith and life in Christ,
For your peace that we find in surrender of our will to yours,
For your peace that comes without our understanding,
THANK YOU, LORD.

For your Spirit that enables us to step forward boldly in faith, rather than hold back in fear and timidity,
For your grace that sets us free to be bold disciples in all that we do,
THANK YOU, LORD.

For all these gifts of joy, love, and peace that fill our hearts to overflowing and sustain us through each day and night,
THANK YOU, LORD!

Just Pray!

Shout with joy to God, all the earth!
  Sing the glory of his name;
  make his praise glorious!
Come and see what God has done,
  how awesome his works in man's behalf!
                              Psalm 66:1-2, 5

Wake up world!
It's a glorious day.

Wake up world!
Time to work and play.

Wake up world!
God is waiting for you today.

Wake up world!
Let God have control of your life.

Wake up world!
Let Jesus be your friend and guide.

Wake up world!
Turn loose of your ego and pride.

Wake up world!
Thank God you're alive!!

Joretta K. Klepfer

And pray in the Spirit on all occasions with all kinds of prayers and requests.
　　　　　　　　　　　　　　　　　　Ephesians 6:18

Just pray!
　　　Wherever you are, whatever you're doing.
Stuck in traffic—
　　　Pray for the other drivers.
Hear a siren—
　　　Pray for the emergency drivers and
　　　the persons they are helping.
Meet a friend—
　　　Pray a prayer of joy and thanksgiving.
Watch a sunset—
　　　Pray a prayer of presence.
Washing dishes—
　　　Thank God for food.
Washing windows—
　　　Thank God for your home.
Brushing your teeth—
　　　Pray for a healthy body
　　　and thank God for the one you have.
Long checkout line—
　　　Pray for patience for you and the clerk.
Angry—
　　　Pray for understanding, tolerance, peace.
Can't sleep—
　　　Count your blessings and thank God for them.
Difficult relationship—
　　　Pray for God's blessing on the other person.
Bedtime—
　　　Thank God for your day.
On waking—
　　　Thank God for the night's rest
　　　and ask his blessing on the new day.

Just Pray!

I call on you, O God, for you will answer me;
give ear to me and hear my prayer.
Show the wonder of your great love...
                                    Psalm 17:6-7a

Just Pray!
Everyday!
> Give God the first minutes.
> Give him the last minutes.
> Give him every minute in between.

Just pray!
He's waiting to hear from you—
> Waiting to hear your confession,
> Waiting to forgive you in his unending mercy.
> Waiting to hear your joys and concerns.
> Waiting to answer your petitions in his own way,
> in his own time.

Just pray!
And feel his love surrounding you,
> Lifting you higher than your limitations,
> Lifting you higher than your hopes and dreams
> Into his arms that will never fail you.

Just pray!
And be at peace.

Joretta K. Klepfer

My prayer for you

May you come to know the Lord
    —in all his
   glory and majesty,
    loving kindness and goodness,
    never ending mercy,
    indescribable peace,
    and unfailing love—
who has redeemed you from sin
and calls you to himself
through Jesus Christ our Savior
and the Holy Spirit, our Counselor.

May you know the joy of life blessed
    with his presence.
May you be drawn to seek him every day!
Just pray!

Joretta Klepfer is an artist by choice, a writer/poet by chance, and a Christian by the grace of God. She and her husband Bob have been married 43 years, have one son, Bob III, and live in Greensboro, North Carolina. Joretta has a BA degree in Mathematics from The University of North Carolina at Greensboro. Her varied career path includes four and one-half years serving as Director of Christian Education and Youth Ministry at First Lutheran Church in Greensboro, North Carolina. Her volunteer experience at First Lutheran extends over 38 years, predominately teaching and working with teenagers but also serving in many other areas, such as Church Council, Stewardship and Worship Committees. She has also served in statewide ministry positions. In addition, Joretta is a self-taught artist, specializing in hand-painted note cards and dinnerware.

Contact Joretta Klepfer through email:
 Joretta.Klepfer@yahoo.com
Order additional copies of
JUST PRAY!
at Tate Publishing, LLC
www.tatepublishing.com.

Tate Publishing & *Enterprises*

Tate Publishing is commited to excellence in the publishing industry. Our staff of highly trained professionals, including editors, graphic designers, and marketing personnel, work together to produce the very finest books available. The company reflects the philosophy established by the founders, based on Psalms 68:11,

"THE LORD GAVE THE WORD AND GREAT WAS THE COMPANY OF THOSE WHO PUBLISHED IT."

If you would like further information, please call
1.888.361.9473
or visit our website
www.tatepublishing.com

TATE PUBLISHING & *Enterprises*, LLC
127 E. Trade Center Terrace
Mustang, Oklahoma 73064 USA